D1289534

SPORTS SCIENCE

THE SCIENCE OF
BASKETBALL

NORMAN D. GRAUBART

PowerKiDS
press.

New York

Published in 2016 by The Rosen Publishing Group, Inc.
29 East 21st Street, New York, NY 10010

First Edition

Editor: Katie Kawa
Book Design: Katelyn Heinle

Photo Credits: Cover Cavan Images/Getty Images; back cover kubais/Shutterstock.com; p. 4 Thearon W. Henderson/Getty Images Sport/Getty Images; p. 5 Doug James/Shutterstock.com; p. 7 tothzoli001/Shutterstock.com; p. 9 The Washington Post/Getty Images; pp. 11, 27 Aspen Photo/Shutterstock.com; p. 13 (left) Stockbyte/Thinkstock.com; pp. 13 (right), 23 Maddie Meyer/Getty Images Sport/Getty Images; p. 14 Vucicevic Milos/Shutterstock.com; p. 15 Scott Halleran/Getty Images Sport/Getty Images; p. 17 Tar_Heel_Rob/Thinkstock.com; p. 19 Jupiterimages/Stockbyte/Getty Images; p. 21 (top) Doug Pensinger/Getty Images Sport/Getty Images; p. 21 (bottom) Hideki Yoshihara/Aflo/Getty Images; p. 25 Andy Lyons/Getty Images Sport/Getty Images; p. 29 Brett Carlsen/Getty Images Sport/Getty Images; p. 30 Monkey Business Images/Shutterstock.com.

Cataloging-in-Publication Data

Graubart, Norman D.
The science of basketball / by Norman D. Graubart.
p. cm. — (Sports science)
Includes index.
ISBN 978-1-4994-1064-8 (pbk.)
ISBN 978-1-4994-1102-7 (6 pack)
ISBN 978-1-4994-1127-0 (library binding)
1. Basketball — Juvenile literature. 2. Sports sciences — Juvenile literature. I. Graubart, Norman D. II. Title.
GV885.1 G735 2016
796.323—d23

Manufactured in the United States of America

CPSIA Compliance Information: Batch #WS15PK: For Further Information contact Rosen Publishing, New York, New York at 1-800-237-9932

Basketball has grown since its invention in 1891 to become one of America's most popular sports. Even though the technology behind the sport has changed over the years, all you need to play basketball are a ball, a hard surface, and one or two baskets. It also helps to have a good understanding of the rules of the sport and the science that makes amazing basketball plays possible.

What does science have to do with basketball? Science helps us answer questions about the sport, such as how to make a perfect basket or what shoes work best on a basketball court.

SCIENCE HELPS US UNDERSTAND HOW COOL PLAYS HAPPEN IN A BASKETBALL GAME. MATH HELPS US BETTER UNDERSTAND THIS SPORT, TOO! STATISTICS, OR STATS, ARE AN IMPORTANT PART OF BASKETBALL. STATS ARE NUMBERS USED TO STAND FOR PIECES OF **INFORMATION**, SUCH AS HOW MANY POINTS A BASKETBALL PLAYER SCORES. THEY ALLOW PEOPLE TO EASILY COMPARE PLAYERS AND TEAMS USING MATH SKILLS.

WNBA

Many of the world's best basketball players are part of the National Basketball Association (NBA), which is the top **professional** basketball league for men in North America. The best female players can be seen in the Women's National Basketball Association (WNBA).

5

All NBA courts are the same shape and size. They're a rectangle, but there are many other shapes within that main rectangle. For example, each NBA court has two 3-point lines, with one on each end of the court. These lines are in the shape of a semicircle, or half-circle.

The basket lies where you would find the center if the semicircle was a whole circle. The distance from a spot on most of the 3-point line to the basket is 23.75 feet (7.24 m). This is called the arc radius. Arc radius measures the distance from the center of a circle to a point on an arc, or part, of that circle. NBA players get an extra point for making a shot at this distance or beyond it.

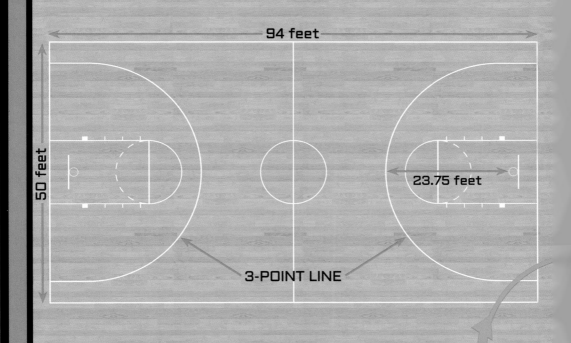

94 feet

50 feet

23.75 feet

3-POINT LINE

FROM THE BASELINE

A BASKETBALL COURT ISN'T WIDE ENOUGH FOR THE 3-POINT LINE TO BE A PERFECT SEMICIRCLE. IT ACTUALLY BECOMES A STRAIGHT LINE AS IT NEARS THE EDGE OF THE COURT, WHICH IS ALSO KNOWN AS THE BASELINE. THIS PART OF THE 3-POINT LINE IS ONLY 22 FEET (6.71 M) FROM THE BASKET. HOWEVER, PLAYERS CAN EASILY GET PUSHED OUT OF BOUNDS THERE, SO THE SHOT IS STILL WORTH AN EXTRA POINT

Physics is a branch of science that can be seen in action throughout a basketball game. This branch of science deals with energy and how it interacts with matter. Forces are an important part of physics and basketball. A force is a push or pull on an object.

Examples of forces can be found all over a basketball court. When a player shoots the basketball, they're pushing the ball with their hands. This is an example of applied force. Applied force is a force one object **exerts** on another.

Normal force is a force that exists between two stable objects. When a basketball player is standing still on the court, the court is exerting an upward force to support them. That force is normal force.

A player needs to use more force to make a 3-point shot because the ball needs to travel a longer distance.

FORCEFUL TRAINING

BASKETBALL PLAYERS WANT TO CREATE AS MUCH FORCE AS THEY CAN WITH THEIR BODY. IN ORDER TO DO THIS, THEY NEED TO BUILD STRONG MUSCLES. A MUSCLE IS A BODY PART THAT PRODUCES MOTION. MUSCLES ARE WHAT ALLOW BASKETBALL PLAYERS TO EXERT THE FORCE NEEDED TO TAKE SHOTS FROM THE 3-POINT LINE AND JUMP HIGH ENOUGH TO BLOCK OTHER PLAYERS' SHOTS.

EXTRA POINT

The force of gravity pulls objects toward Earth's center. Gravity is what makes a basketball come down after a player shoots it into the air.

Basketball players are known for being tall. They also often have a lot of muscle mass. The heavier a player is, the more mass he or she has. Mass is how much stuff there is in an object. Mass is like weight, but an object's weight depends on gravity. A basketball player might weigh 200 pounds (90.7 kg) on Earth, but they would weigh something else on another planet that has a different amount of gravity. The player's mass, however, will always be the same.

Momentum is mass in motion. The more mass an object has, the harder it will be for it to slow down and eventually stop. It takes more force to change the motion of an object with more mass, so it's harder for bigger basketball players to start running, stop, and change direction.

Point guards are generally shorter basketball players who have less mass than other players. This means they can stop quickly to change direction and pass the ball. They also need less energy to run quickly than players with more mass.

A BASKETBALL PLAYER'S MOMENTUM CAN BE FOUND USING MATH. MULTIPLY THE PLAYER'S MASS BY THEIR VELOCITY, AND THE ANSWER IS THEIR MOMENTUM. WHAT'S VELOCITY? IT'S THE MEASUREMENT OF THE RATE AT WHICH AN OBJECT CHANGES ITS POSITION. VELOCITY IS LIKE SPEED, BUT THE DIRECTION AN OBJECT IS MOVING ALSO MATTERS WHEN MEASURING VELOCITY.

EXTRA POINT

The momentum of an object at rest is 0.

The surface of a basketball court can make all the difference in how a game is played. Basketball players dribble, or bounce, the ball as they move. A ball will bounce with the most force on a hard surface. Soft surfaces **absorb** more of the ball's energy, so it doesn't bounce back with as much force. This is why basketballs don't bounce very high on grass.

Professional and **collegiate** basketball teams play on hardwood floors. A hardwood floor is a very strong and smooth surface, so it doesn't absorb too much of the ball's energy when it's dribbled. This makes it the ideal surface for basketball games.

Hardwood floors are only used for indoor basketball courts. Water and sunlight can ruin the surface.

CONCRETE COURTS

OUTDOOR BASKETBALL COURTS ARE COMMONLY MADE WITH CONCRETE OR ASPHALT, WHICH IS ALSO KNOWN AS BLACKTOP. THESE TWO **MATERIALS** ARE STRONG AND HARD. THEY DON'T ABSORB A LOT OF ENERGY FROM THE FORCE OF THE BALL HITTING THE SURFACE. BOTH OF THESE MATERIALS ARE ALSO ABLE TO WITHSTAND HARSH WEATHER.

You may think professional basketball players wear special shoes because they look cool. Actually, these shoes help basketball players perform better. The material on the bottom of their shoes helps them run fast on slippery hardwood courts. This is because of a force called friction.

Friction is any force that resists motion. It occurs when an object moves across a surface. Why is friction good for basketball players? Often, they have to run quickly down the court, and friction keeps them from sliding on the smooth surface of the hardwood floor. The bottoms of basketball shoes are **designed** to increase friction between the shoe and the floor. This increased friction slows the movement of the shoe over the floor enough to keep players from slipping.

EXTRA POINT

The technology used to make and design basketball shoes has greatly improved since the sport's earliest days. The most advanced materials are used to make shoes as light as possible to increase a player's velocity while still being strong enough to absorb much of the force when the player lands after jumping.

CLEAN IT UP!

BECAUSE THE FLOOR OF A BASKETBALL COURT IS NATURALLY SLIPPERY, WORKERS TRY TO KEEP IT FROM BECOMING MORE SLIPPERY BY QUICKLY WIPING UP ANY WATER THAT MAY SPILL ON IT—OR EVEN EXTRA SWEAT FROM PLAYERS' BODIES! WATER AND SWEAT ACT AS LUBRICANTS, OR **SUBSTANCES** THAT REDUCE FRICTION. IF FRICTION IS REDUCED ON THE COURT, PLAYERS CAN SLIP AND GET INJURED, OR HURT.

The technology used to make basketball shoes keeps getting better. This is important because the right shoes can keep players from getting injured.

BALL BASICS

The friction between an NBA player's hands and the basketball wears down the surface of the ball over time. This is because NBA basketballs are made of leather, which softens as it's exposed to heat and friction.

A basketball is just a piece of material without the air inside it. Air is pumped into a basketball through a tiny hole in the ball. As more air gets pumped into the ball, the air pressure inside it increases. Air pressure is the force exerted on a surface, such as the inside of a basketball, by air **molecules**. If the air pressure inside a basketball is too low, it won't bounce very high. It also won't hold the round shape basketballs are known to have.

COMPOSITE CONCERNS

IN 2006, THE NBA BEGAN USING COMPOSITE BASKETBALLS, WHICH ARE BASKETBALLS MADE OF DIFFERENT MAN-MADE MATERIALS THAT ARE MADE TO FEEL LIKE LEATHER. THESE BALLS ARE CHEAPER THAN LEATHER BALLS AND AREN'T AS AFFECTED BY FRICTION. HOWEVER, THE PLAYERS PREFERRED THE LEATHER BALL, SO COMPOSITE BASKETBALLS ARE NO LONGER USED IN THE NBA.

Leather basketballs, such as official NBA basketballs, should only be used indoors.

EXTRA POINT

Basketballs made of rubber are commonly used on outdoor courts. Rubber is more durable than leather, so it's used on rougher court surfaces, such as concrete.

WHAT A DRAG!

Air pressure isn't just experienced inside a container such as a basketball. It can be felt all around us as the force exerted by molecules in the air. When an object moves through the air, the air molecules collide with the surface of the object and slow its motion. This is known as air resistance, or drag.

During a basketball game, the ball is often in the air. As players pass or shoot the ball, it moves through the air and is affected by air resistance. The air resistance an object experiences increases as its velocity increases. A steady increase in velocity is called acceleration.

PLAYING IN THIN AIR

IF YOU PLAY BASKETBALL OUTSIDE AT A LOCATION IN THE MOUNTAINS, THE BALL WILL EXPERIENCE LESS AIR RESISTANCE. THIS IS BECAUSE THERE ARE FEWER MOLECULES IN THE AIR AT HIGHER ELEVATIONS. IF THERE ARE FEWER AIR MOLECULES, THERE'S LESS AIR PRESSURE PUSHING AGAINST THE BALL. IF YOU THREW A BASKETBALL WITH THE SAME FORCE ON AN OUTDOOR COURT AT SEA LEVEL AND AN OUTDOOR COURT IN THE MOUNTAINS, IT WOULD GO FARTHER IN THE MOUNTAINS.

A special branch of science deals with objects moving through air and air moving around objects. It's called aerodynamics.

EXTRA POINT

Air resistance is sometimes called air friction because it's a force that works to slow down an object moving through the air.

Every shot a basketball player takes is affected by air resistance.

Much of the action on a basketball court takes place around the basket, which is sometimes called the net. The circular, metal hoop that holds up the net is called the rim. Basketball rims have a diameter of 18 inches (45.7 cm). The diameter is the measurement of any straight line that passes through the center of a circle. If the diameter of the rim was even an inch larger, then it would be a lot easier to make a shot. This is because a circle expands, or gets bigger, in every direction as its diameter increases.

The rim is **attached** to the backboard, and it's designed to bend when players pull on it. Otherwise, the rim would break during a slam dunk!

Sometimes basketball players dunk the ball with so much force that they break the backboard!

EXTRA POINT

The backboard is the upright part of a basket behind the net. It needs to be made of strong material because the ball hits it throughout the game. NBA backboards are generally made of glass that's been treated with special chemicals or created using extreme heat and cold to make it stronger.

SLAM DUNK SCIENCE

BASKETBALL PLAYERS USE A LOT OF FORCE TO JUMP HIGH ENOUGH TO DUNK THE BALL. THAT FORCE GENERALLY COMES FROM THEIR LEG MUSCLES. A SLAM DUNK EXERTS A LARGE AMOUNT OF FORCE ON THE RIM, SO ENGINEERS HAVE CREATED RIMS DESIGNED TO BOUNCE BACK AFTER TAKING ON LARGE AMOUNTS OF FORCE.

←18 INCHES→

ACTIONS AND REACTIONS

Instead of aiming for the net when you shoot a basketball, try aiming for the backboard. If the ball hits the backboard in the right spot, it can fall in the rim. If the ball is thrown with too much force, then it will bounce far from the net. This is because of a scientific law called Newton's third law of motion.

EXTRA POINT

Sir Isaac Newton was a British scientist who lived from 1643 to 1727. He's considered the father of modern physics.

basketball example	action and reaction
dribbling	When the ball hits the ground, the ground pushes back on the ball with equal, upward force.
missed shot	When a missed shot hits the rim, the rim pushes back on the ball with equal force.
falling	When a player falls on the court, the floor pushes back on the player's body with equal force.

This chart shows some more examples of Newton's third law of motion at work in a basketball game.

Newton's third law of motion states for every action, there's an equal and opposite **reaction**. If you hit the backboard with the basketball, the backboard will push back on the ball with same amount of force. Players have to learn to shoot with the proper aim and amount of force to avoid having their shots bounce away from the net.

NEWTON'S FIRST LAW

NEWTON'S THREE LAWS OF MOTION ARE STILL STUDIED TODAY. NEWTON'S FIRST LAW OF MOTION STATES THAT AN OBJECT AT REST STAYS AT REST AND AN OBJECT IN MOTION STAYS IN MOTION WITH THE SAME VELOCITY UNLESS ACTED UPON BY AN OUTSIDE FORCE. FOR EXAMPLE, A BASKETBALL STAYS IN MOTION WHEN IT'S BEING PASSED UNTIL THE FORCE EXERTED BY ANOTHER PLAYER'S HANDS STOPS IT.

AMAZING ACCELERATION

Newton's second law of motion is all about acceleration. It states that an object's acceleration can be affected by the forces acting on the object and the mass of the object. If the force acting on an object increases, the object's acceleration increases. Imagine a basketball player passing the ball to their teammate. If that player passes the same ball a second time with more force, the ball will accelerate more quickly and reach a higher velocity.

Newton's second law also states that, as the mass of an object increases, its acceleration decreases. This is why basketball shoes are designed to be as light as possible. A shoe that's too heavy could add to a player's overall mass enough to affect their ability to accelerate quickly.

SLOWING IT DOWN

THE GAME OF BASKETBALL MOVES FAST! IT CAN BE HARD TO SEE IF RULES WERE BROKEN, WHO MADE THE BALL GO OUT OF BOUNDS, OR IF A SHOT IS WORTH 2 OR 3 POINTS DURING AN NBA GAME. VIDEO REPLAY TECHNOLOGY ALLOWS NBA OFFICIALS TO WATCH CERTAIN PLAYS AGAIN, USING DIFFERENT CAMERA ANGLES AND SLOWING DOWN THE ACTION TO MAKE SURE THE RIGHT CALLS ARE MADE.

EXTRA POINT

If the forces acting on an object are balanced, it's not accelerating. This state is called equilibrium. If a basketball player is standing still, the forces acting on them are balanced.

Force and mass play an important role in how quickly basketball players are able to accelerate as they run down the court.

Energy can't be created or destroyed. It can only change forms. When you dribble a basketball, you **transfer** energy from your body to the ball.

Objects that are in motion have kinetic energy, or energy used to do work. Objects that have stored energy have potential energy. When a basketball is resting in your hand above the ground, it has potential energy. When the ball falls to the ground, it has kinetic energy.

When a basketball moves through the air, it has both potential and kinetic energy. This is because the ball turns more of its potential energy into kinetic energy as it accelerates. The ball always has the same amount of total energy. That energy can be stored or used to do work.

This team of basketball players has a lot of potential energy in them. As they play, they'll turn much of it into kinetic energy.

ENERGY FROM FOOD

BASKETBALL PLAYERS NEED A LOT OF ENERGY. THIS MEANS THEY NEED TO EAT FOODS WITH A LOT OF POTENTIAL ENERGY THAT CAN BE CHANGED INTO KINETIC ENERGY BY THEIR BODY. COMPLEX CARBOHYDRATES ARE SUBSTANCES FOUND IN FOOD THAT GIVE PEOPLE LONG-LASTING ENERGY. FOODS RICH IN COMPLEX CARBOHYDRATES INCLUDE WHOLE-GRAIN BREAD AND BROWN RICE.

EXTRA POINT

When a player dribbles a basketball, some of the potential energy is changed to heat and sound energy. The friction between the ball and floor produces small amounts of heat. We experience the sound energy as the familiar noise of a ball bouncing on the ground.

LOUD ARENAS

The crowds at basketball games can produce a lot of sound energy. You can picture a sound as a wave rippling through the air. Sometimes, the wave keeps going through the air without hitting anything. It begins to lose energy the farther away it moves from its source.

Indoor basketball arenas have walls and ceilings that sound waves bounce, or reflect, off of. The sound waves reflect so many times that it creates an effect called reverberation. Sound waves that reverberate repeat for longer than sound waves that don't. This means the sounds that come from those waves last longer.

The study of sound is called acoustics. Some people design acoustics for big arenas. They're called sound engineers.

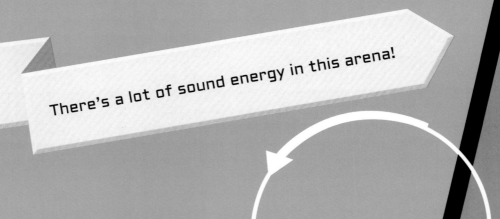

There's a lot of sound energy in this arena!

SOUND LEVELS

WHEN WE TALK ABOUT SOUNDS, WE OFTEN TALK ABOUT THEM IN TERMS OF LOUDNESS. HOWEVER, SCIENTISTS DON'T MEASURE SOUNDS BY HOW LOUD THEY ARE, BECAUSE DIFFERENT PEOPLE HEAR SOUNDS DIFFERENTLY. INSTEAD, THEY MEASURE SOUND BY ITS INTENSITY, WHICH IS THE AMOUNT OF ENERGY IN A SOUND WAVE. THE INTENSITY OF A GIVEN SOUND IS CALLED ITS SOUND LEVEL.

THE CARRIER DOME, SYRACUSE, NEW YORK

EXTRA POINT

All sounds—from the cheering of fans to the swish of a basketball going through the net—are produced by some kind of motion, or kinetic energy.

The best basketball players are skilled and smart. They know how to use science to perform at their best in every game. You can use science on the basketball court, too.

If you want to avoid slipping on a hardwood court, be sure to have shoes that increase friction between your feet and the floor. If you're playing in a place with lower air pressure, be sure to adjust the force of your shot. Finally, remember how momentum affects you as you run down the court. Science is always around you, whether you're playing or watching basketball!

GLOSSARY

absorb: To take in or soak up.

arena: A building for sports and other forms of entertainment that has a large central area surrounded by seats.

attached: Joined together.

collegiate: Relating to a college or its students.

design: To make a plan for how to make something.

exert: To put forth.

information: Knowledge or facts about something.

material: Something from which something else can be made.

molecule: The smallest part of something.

professional: Having to do with the job someone does for a living.

reaction: The force that an object subjected to an outside force exerts in the opposite direction.

substance: Matter of a certain kind.

transfer: To move or carry from one person, place, or thing to another.

WEBSITES

Due to the changing nature of Internet links, PowerKids Press has developed an online list of websites related to the subject of this book. This site is updated regularly. Please use this link to access the list: www.powerkidslinks.com/spsci/bball